Leverage Your List

The Secret to Growing Your Small Business

By Chris Ripley

Here's What's Inside...

Introduction

Leverage Your List!
Waldorf, Maryland
August 2014

During many years of helping small businesses grow I have seen firsthand what happens when they don't create or maintain a good customer list. It always makes me sad to see a three generation family business go out of business because they can't reach their best customers at any given time.

I was fortunate to be told when I started my business I needed to have a list and keep it in a place where I could use it to keep my current customers and get new ones. I have been showing clients how to leverage their customer list for years.

The following is a transcription where I'm interviewed sharing my ideas about getting your list together and using it to grow your business.

Enjoy the book!

I hope this book provides the seed for you to start your list and I hope it changes the way you look at where your next wave of business is going to come from.

To Your Success!

Chris Ripley

Leverage Your List!

Susan: Good afternoon this is Susan Austin and I'm super excited to be here today with Chris Ripley to discuss his thoughts and ideas on how small business owners can grow their business. Welcome Chris.

Chris: Thank you very much, glad to be here Susan.

Why Don't More Business Owners Have a Thriving Business?

Susan: Let's start off with why you wanted to write this book Chris?

Chris: When I meet with small business owners one of the first questions I ask them is do they have a list of their clients and prospects? Very honestly more often than not I usually get a soft no, a squishy no or a definite no. Some might have a box of business cards in a drawer somewhere or they may keep a few names in Excel but when pressed it's usually outdated information.

Lots of small businesses are just not taking advantage of what I perceive is the number one opportunity for them; to have an updated list of clients and prospects and be able to use that list to generate more business. I wanted to shine a light on this key business component a lot of business owners just miss.

Susan: Why do you think that is Chris? Why don't they have a list?

Chris: That's a good question. Very often the business is busy delivering the product and services of their business so they get busy in working in the business and if they don't setup a system to capture the names it never gets done. Creating a list is a key component but it's often overlooked possibly due to perceived time constraints. I'm going to show the business owner later in the book how to automate things so the list building is automated. Also, to be frank, I think a lot of business owners have never been educated on how important it is for them to have a list of their customers. No one's done the math for them and if their people aren't trained to ask for the information often times in the busy-ness of getting through the week it gets overlooked.

Susan: What happens when the small business owners don't have a customer list? What is the fallout from that?

Chris: That's going to mean less business and in some cases maybe going out of business. They say 80 percent of small businesses fail within the first 5 years and certainly as a small business observer in my community and having interactions with people I often see these businesses go out of business.

There was a local franchise here where I live where it allows you to come in and make your own meals. It was pretty cool. You make 10 meals or however many you want, for the month. My wife and I did it a few times and not once did the business owner follow up with us. They had our information on file but they didn't use it to try to get us to come back in. Right now it's an empty store-front.

You see this time and time again. Business owners often think having their doors open for business is enough. Or they think they advertise in Valpak so that should be enough. It's not. In today's busy world you need to be able to reach your clients to be top-of-mind. It's critical for business success.

In fact, here's another example to highlight this. There's a vacuum and sewing machine shop around the corner from me that has been in business over 25 years. It was once a thriving business with 8 to 10 employees. Now it's just the shop owner and a part time employee to give him a break and a day off every once in a while. He is clearly struggling. I stopped in and sure enough the closest thing he had to a customer list was boxes of receipts by year in the back. And upon further review most of those didn't have much more than a name on them. No email address, no phone numbers, and no physical address. The business owner saw no specific reasons to capture that information.

This gentleman has been in business for 25 years and never accumulated any information on his clients and prospects. He was basically relying on the walk in business to his shop. If he had been building a client list from day one think about how big of a list he would have now after 25 years? He's met and worked with thousands of clients over the years but has no way of reaching them. It's a shame when you stop and think about it.

Susan: He has no way of reaching any of his clients to let them know about new vacuum cleaner models? He can't reach out and try and get more business?

Chris: Right and those are the easiest clients to get. The easiest clients to get are going to be the folks who have already been to your store. They've made the leap. They already know and like you. That's why malls are so popular because in mall stores you don't have to open the door per se; you get so much foot traffic. But when you're in a strip center like this store was every person who makes the effort to open your door and walk in and interact with you is clearly there for a reason and this is a person you should be adding to your customer list. And in fact, doing that is very easy to setup and do. Yet again so many miss this very important step.

Susan: I can see this could mean the difference between struggling and thriving. What are some of the options the business owner has for capturing this information Chris?

Chris: There are many different ways. You often hear business owners who use Google AdWords who try it once and say it doesn't work for them. They'll say Google AdWords is no good, "We tried it and it didn't work."

When you dig a little deeper you find out they were sending the Google Adwords traffic to the homepage of their website. However, there is no place on their website which is easy to spot where the potential client can engage in the next step of the sales process, whatever that might be for that particular business. If it's an irrigation system company maybe you offer a free estimate for the customer, so you would have a form on the home page where somebody could give you their contact information and you could call them and set up a free estimate for them.

It's unfortunate a lot of small business owners aren't doing some of these basic things. A lot of these things can be automated. That's one of the cool things about this with Internet technology today much of it can be automated.

How to Start Building Your Customer List...

Susan: What do you mean automated? I'm thinking of the vacuum cleaner owner who owns the strip mall store. What could he do to create a list?

Chris: Most point-of-sale software has a way to capture email addresses every time you interact with somebody. It can be very low key to ask for someone's email address.

Ask them, "Would you like to join our list and we'll let you know when we're having sales, or special offers? It's a very common question and if they are there buying something from you, chances are they want what you are offering so it's a very natural question. They say the capture rate on asking for email addresses, depending on how good you are, could be as low as 20% but as high as 80%.

That is one thing our vacuum cleaner store owner could do. Just start asking for email addresses of the customers he's already working with. I was just cleaning out my office, trying to get rid of some stuff when I found an old book I received from Constant Contact. It's similar to a guest registry. The small business owner could just put that on the sales counter and ask guests to sign the registry. It might collect dust but if you put it there and ask people to sign a guest registry and tell them you will let them know about upcoming events and new merchandize that comes in or when you buy vacuum bags. Maybe sometimes you have sales on vacuum bags so they can come in and buy them when they are on sale.

Maybe you want to do a class on how to get the most value out of your vacuum cleaner and have your carpets last longer. You could have people sign up for the class and capture their information and then ask them if they would also like to be on your email list. There are lots of ways to do this. You can have a form on your website, you could ask in person. Another startling fact, and I've seen this many places, is they say that 80% percent of trade show leads don't receive follow-ups.

The first thing I would recommend to any business that's not capturing names and addresses and phone numbers and email addresses is they start right now. Even if you just do it on a pad of paper and you put a couple of lines there, just use a ruler so it looks a little bit nicer and put it on a clip board and ask people to sign up. You don't want to necessarily have the opportunity for people to see other people's email addresses so maybe you do a page for each person or you figure something out. This is worth it. This is going to be worth a lot of money to you. In fact, I propose your list could someday be the biggest asset for your business.

If you're using your list solely for email you'll get a big return on it. They say that email marketing gets 30 to 40 times return on investment. For every $100 you invest in email marketing you should be able to get $3,000 to $4,000 in business from it. I'm not afraid to say that. I think there's no question that if you do it and do it well you will see results. I see it happen with client after client after client.

Susan: The small business owner who doesn't have a list so they're not able then to leverage their list and stay in touch with their clients and get repeat business from them; as a result they have to then spend 10 times more on advertising to keep new clients coming in the door month after month?

Chris: That's right. And that's not going to be a successful strategy in the long term. I read a statistic recently which stated it's 7 times more expensive to get a new customer than to keep an existing one. Think about that for a moment. How much money is the business owner losing by not having an up to date customer list?

One of the biggest questions I get from people is how much should I spend on advertising, what percent of sales? You have to look at your industry and make a decision based on your margins and that sort of thing but when you're able to use a list to proactively solicit business, if you're a restaurant and you know that Monday nights are notoriously slow, so Monday afternoon you send out an email to your client list and you get 7 additional diners in that night.

If you don't have the ability to invite your customers in the door you're going to have to use Valpak or other ways to reach clients, which is a lot more expensive than sending a timely email reminding people of a special you are running.

Especially with a restaurant, if you've been to a restaurant and had a good experience and they offer you a discount through an incentive to return you're going to come back again and eventually you'll develop a very strong relationship with those clients. They will appreciate that you thought of them and cared enough to let them know. If you don't have the customer list to leverage you're going to have to think of alternatives to generate business. And often those alternatives are more expensive.

Take direct mail for example. Doing every door direct mail is very inexpensive (about 17 cents per piece) but if you have your own list you'll pay 28 cents. For less than double you're getting people who already know your business and don't have to be pushed hard to come back. Even when you put media against media you're going to do much better with your own list. You can target Facebook users from your email list. Now you should also do some other things where you go off your list but having that business that you get from your list is going to be what keeps you afloat and then where you go trolling for new customers is when you do more of that other type of marketing.

Susan: How long does list building take?

Chris: It can take no time at all actually. When you think about the vacuum cleaner gentleman, for example, it's going to take him just a few minutes to ask a couple of questions of his clients while they are making their purchase. That's a relatively insignificant amount of time. There's no better time than the present to start with your list building. If he just did that simple thing it wouldn't take that much time.

If you're a startup business and you are looking to build your list you're going to have to invest a little bit of time into it.

You're going to have to, especially if you're targeted to the business to business market, go to chamber of commerce events and networking events and things like that and collect business cards and talk to people and put those people on the business cards on your list and start building it that way.

There are many places that you can buy a list.

I often buy lists from InfoUSA.com; I've been dealing with them for a long time. You could go on their website and pick your list, business to business (B2B) or business to consumer (B2C), you can choose demographics and geography and income and even get lists of new home owners if you would like. You can get business and industry categories. If you were a new business and you were starting off locally and you were B2B based and you wanted to get a list of all the businesses that do a million dollars or more within 25 miles of your home base you can get that list.

You're going to pay for it but I have never seen where it's not easy money, where you invest in the list and you're pretty much certain you're going to get a return on investment. It's hard to buy emails and I know people who do this but I try to stay away from it. When you buy that list, first you're going to have to start working on direct mail and create a direct mail piece for these people which is going to cost you a little bit more but then again we're talking about starting at ground zero here. You're going to have to figure out a way to capture their attention and get them to respond with the free report.

Let's say you're an attorney and you are just getting started. Many attorneys are coming out of law school and it's hard to find jobs with firms so they're trying to start up on their own. If you were an attorney in that position and you were going to do business law, you would buy a list of businesses you think might be interested in your services. You could prepare a free report with the 7 things every small business owner needs to know about the law but is afraid to ask; something along those lines. It's pretty easy and inexpensive to do.

You could put the free report offering on a post card which directs them to your website or to a landing page and there they would get the free report. Then you could follow up with them. That would be one way to create your list if you are starting a new business.

Susan: I can't imagine having hundreds or eventually thousands of your clients who have purchased from you over the last 5 to 10 years wouldn't be extremely valuable to the small business owner.

Chris: It's valuable even if you're a real estate agent with a practice and you're selling 10, 15, to 20 houses a year. You want to retire and you have a list of a couple hundred people you have sold houses to or shown houses to, this is just from one agent. You can find another real estate agent who is aggressive who might buy the list from you or you allow them to work the list, retain ownership of the list and you receive 20 or 25 percent of whatever they sell. That would be just one small example.

In a broader example, I have a couple of clients that I'm working with right now who are thinking about selling their business in the future. They're asking me to help them build a list and use that list to generate more business. If you have a great list and you're working the list on a regular basis and you can show somebody that every month you get 12 new customers on the list or from the efforts that you're doing on Google AdWords and accumulating those people on to your list. That's going to add tremendous value to your business.

How to Store Your Customer List...

Susan: Let's talk about how the small business can get started with their list. You've mentioned a couple of ways but for someone who's brand new to this where should they start?

Chris: They could start with something as simple as Excel and use that and then move on to other tools. Excel or Google Apps are probably about the simplest level that you could start. You can look at online places to keep your list. That would be maybe something like Constant Contact. Recently Constant Contact added a good CRM element. It's the opportunity to have your contact list, email, surveys, events all in one place and it starts off at $20 a month so it's relatively inexpensive.

While Constant Contact was originally an email service, it now has a contact management tool so that you can add anybody in there whether you have their email address or not. I think it's a great choice for small businesses.

For bigger businesses that may have outgrown Constant Contact I recommend Infusionsoft. That would be the best place for them to go. Pick what you would like on the tools out there. There's CapsuleCRM.com another online solution that I looked at before I moved to Infusionsoft about three years ago. Also consider Salesforce.com.

I wouldn't recommend trying to run your list in your email client (Outlook, Gmail, etc.), it just doesn't give you enough flexibility and when you're looking at where you want to keep your list and if you're going to use email marketing you want to make sure that you'll have a tool that will give you metrics. You want to know things like how many emails were opened. If you have any links in your email you want to know "are people clicking on them?"

If you send out an email with a link and 12 people click on the link, those people might be 12 prospects for that product or service that the link was connected to.

Pick where you want to put your list that would be the first thing that I would say. Then the next thing you'd want to do is start accumulating information in any way that you can. Run a contest if you'd like to capture people's names and addresses (beware – when you run contests you will get people on your list who want to win something but have no interest in your product or service). When you go to a trade show and you get those business cards make sure you take them back and at least get them transcribed into Excel. For people that are collecting business cards for their list there are also tools that you could add to your smart phone that enable you to take a picture of the business card and then it's transcribed electronically, or a real person in a foreign land transcribes it.

Susan: For those of us who are new to this can you give us a layman's version of what Infusionsoft is?

Chris: Infusionsoft is the all-in-one sales and marketing automation system for small business. Basically, it is online software with very close to everything a small business would need to manage their customer database and to communicate with their customers on a regular basis. You can manage your sales team and sell online with Infusionsoft. It has a robust developer marketplace where people have tools that you could add on to Infusionsoft. If you're in the B2B world and you're inviting people to webinars you could automate the webinar process. Having webinars is another great way to grow your list.

Infusionsoft for a small businesses doing half a million dollars or more or solo entrepreneurs who're doing less it's almost a must have tool to manage their business. Infusionsoft takes a little bit of time to learn and it's an investment. Constant Contact is $20 a month; Infusionsoft is $200 a month. Infusionsoft can do a lot more for you but you pay for that ability. There are many businesses that can do fine with Constant Contact and there are others that might need Infusionsoft, depending on what industry and what the business owner wants to invest in their list.

Susan: What about the business owner who has a list but isn't leveraging it well, what do you recommend they do?

Chris: The person that has a list and doesn't use it is the second most prevalent person I see in the small business world. When I said that 50 percent of the small businesses probably have no list at all or a very soft list and then the next ones would be those that are smart enough to know that they need to collect that information but don't know what to do with it. I've come across people who have email marketing tools that they've been paying for every month and they've got their list in there but they haven't used it in a year, 2, 3, 4 even 5 years.

When you have that, as with almost anything in the business world, you have to start doing things and you can't make excuses. The first thing, I've done this with many businesses, if they have that Excel spreadsheet and they've been accumulating email addresses but they haven't done anything with it and we put it into Constant Contact; generally within the first 2 or 3 emails they'll start seeing positive results, sometimes even more.

I once worked with a tutoring store where they helped students with SAT preparation and school problems. He was one of those people that had been accumulating the email addresses but really hadn't done anything with it. We put the list into Constant Contact and on the third email that we sent out one of the parents who was on the list forwarded it to another parent because they had been discussing their child's need for an SAT prep program. This person had already been through it and was very happy with it. The person signed this kid up for a $2400 SAT prep class. He paid $240 for a years worth of Constant Contact. So that's 10 times return on ONE email.

How to Leverage an Old Email List...

Susan: Dean Jackson's favorite email to send to old email lists is less than 9 words long: "Are you still interested in buying X?" "Do you still need tutoring in math?" "Are you still looking to buy a home in Scottsdale?" Very simple emails to an old list can generate a lot of sales.

Chris: No question at all. It's not that complicated, it's a pretty simple email and an email like that can maybe also help you clean up a little bit of deadwood on your list. Because maybe a few people will write back and say no, I've moved, leave me alone.

I think that's an important part of your list; list hygiene and just making sure that the people that are on your list are interested in your product or service, so think about the other side of it trying to keep your list clean. Other things that I wanted to cover because not only can you do it with email marketing but if you have a list of addresses do try some direct mail marketing because you'll get a decent return on investment on that as well. I mean you still should be able to see 1 to 3 percent response from direct mail marketing and some people aren't online, some people aren't on email.

Direct mail marketing gets a bad rap because people don't do it right, not because it's not an effective marketing tactic. When I say do it right, you've got to make sure that you have some sort of headline that will draw people's attention to the problem that you solved for them, if you're an exterminator you want to make it look ugly, pictures of the bedbugs and that sort of thing and termites chewing away at your foundation or whatever it might be. Make sure to use that on the list of old pest control customers who don't do business with you anymore, give them an incentive to come back.

Make sure that you do a good job of getting their attention to begin with (the headline) and make sure that you give them an idea of what the next step might be. That would be a good direct mail piece and that's really how most of your marketing should be anyway.

Another way might be taking your email list and putting it into Facebook and if people use the same email address on Facebook as you have you can advertise to them or market to them on their newsfeed. That's a great tool to use. Do it at the same time you do an email; do Facebook also then when people are online - they might see it twice.

Getting social media involved is a little bit more advanced but not that complicated. We haven't talked a lot about it but social media also presents another opportunity to grow your list and use the current list that you have or try to build another list. One of the things that I caution people on, this is a blog post that I just did this week. It is a re-occurring theme at Infusioncon, a conference where about 2400 small business owners attend to learn about improving the small business and using Infusionsoft. I also attended Social Media Marketing World in March and it was a theme that occurred there as well, "don't build your house on rented land" (visit my blog at www.strategic-marketing-group.com).

If you're going to use Facebook to help grow your list, just make sure that's not the only place you use to help grow your list and you're doing things in your store or you're using other tools, you're getting lists from your website or you're attending networking events, have other strategies because if you build your whole list building strategy on Facebook and they decide to change things you can really be in trouble that way.

Susan: It all starts with having a list! You can use all these other ways of reaching your clients but you've got to have the list to start!

Chris: It opens up tons of opportunity for you. One of the best customers I've ever had, a lawn care company, when I started to work for them they had a great list and they were already using it. With them we were quickly able to do some advanced strategies with Google AdWords and their website and use Constant Contact a lot more aggressively. We were able to do surveys in Constant Contact, these people have been so good at managing their list that when we did the survey we sent it out to their 2,000 customers and we got over 400 responses, a 20 percent response. We got great information that we were able to use for marketing for the next year.

We learned a lot about what customers liked, why they chose us, etc. This is a type of survey that any business could do at any time but because they had the basic stuff under control when I started working with them we were able to take it to the next level relatively quickly. This is a very healthy growing business. That's because when they started 26 years ago they knew that they needed to have a list. Their list is as old as their business. They still have 4 customers that were with them when they first started their business.

Susan: Very good example Chris.

Chris: That's a list building success story. With this company we also built a new website and on the home page is a request for a free lawn care estimate. In the first month that we had it up they got 120 leads from it. These were new leads as they had never used this channel before. They certainly didn't get 120 the year before with the set up that they had.

Susan: Do you want to share ideas Chris for maintaining the list? You alluded to it earlier about how to keep your customer list clean.

Chris: When you decide to have a good list and you use it to grow your business you should commit some time to list maintenance as well. We'll start with email. If you're using an email service you'll see bounces - email addresses that are no good for one reason or another.

It could be that that person closed that email address. It could be that that person doesn't work there anymore. Usually your email client will tell you what the reasons are. Then I recommend where there are situations sometimes you'll find that you put in an email address and you forgot to put the dot in so it didn't have dot com on it so that's the error that caused the bounce. We'll often call people to get the correct email address when it bounces.

Take the time to do that, either you or have an administrative person do that for you but keep your list clean by eliminating or updating your bounces and make sure that you try to limit the number of bounces that you have and keep that a very low number. I was just looking at the beginning of the month, we have a list that we send out about 2200 emails at a time and we had 60 bounces so I thought it was time that we try to dig in to that a little bit more.

We send a monthly newsletter to our top 400 prospects, a printed newsletter. We print it out and put a little bit of time into it. I started doing this about 3 years ago and it's one of the best decisions I've ever made. I get higher value clients from it. I once went in to a prospect's office that turned in to a client and he had my printed newsletter on his bulletin board. When you're sending 400 a month we'll have 3 or 4 or 5 or 6 return to us every month because businesses close or they change locations and the forwarding expires and they never tell us until it starts getting bounced back if the forwarding has expired.

The simple point is, keep your list up to date!

We do our best there as well to make sure that if we can't get a hold of a business or it looks like they've moved locally, I try to find their new location, maybe go online to check. Other things that you can do, other advanced strategies, not too advanced would be to send your list to companies that actually do clean it up for you. Not only can they clean it up and make sure you have the right addresses and zip codes and all that sort of thing but they can even do psychographics on it.

If you have names and addresses especially B2B and B2C your list can tell you what your customer profile is. If they have the information or they have the addresses and can cross reference that with the demographic data, then from the demographic data they're able to infer some things about where these people shop, what type of things they look for, etc. They can tell you this information by percentages for your customer list. You can send out your list and you'll find out what your top 3 or 4 customer profiles are, find out maybe where you're missing opportunities and where to target.

These are more advanced strategies when you have a list already. You can learn a lot from your list. One of the best places to do that is Facebook. Facebook knows more about us than pretty much anybody, maybe even than the IRS.

From the list that you build of people who like your business page on Facebook you can go into the insights. You could go into Facebook and you can learn what portion of your list is men, what percent is women, how old they are, you can dig in where they live, you can dig in deeper, you can find out what they like, are they people that like Harley-Davidsons, what are they like? That'll give you an idea maybe to position yourself near these other things that people like.

If you see that a lot of your customers shop at Macy's and you see Macy's advertising in a particular way they've probably invested a lot of money to learn that that's the place where they should be maybe you should be there as well. Those are the more advanced things that you could learn. You could learn it from Facebook. You could learn it from getting a psychographic profile of your list. Those are a little bit more advanced methods but right for your business.

Why List Segmentation Can Make You More Money...

Susan: Do you recommend the business owner keep one list or should they have different lists depending on categories?

Chris: We haven't talked about segmenting your list and I'm glad you brought that up. You want to try to be able to segment your list to how you run your business. If you have certain profiles of customers you want to be able to go to that profile in your list and identify those customers and then market to them with something that will appeal to them. If you find that you have customers that only buy when things are on sale they might not be the customers that you want to send a direct mail piece to about a new expensive item that you might be selling but then if you have people that have bought all of your high end stuff that's definitely something that you would want to do.

Whenever you would like to learn where people came from, go back to the vacuum cleaner gentleman. When I met with this gentleman for the first time, I was there for almost 2 hours because he had to get up and help customers in between talking with me because he was the only guy there. He had, vacuum cleaners and sewing machines and he had people, a couple of people that came in to buy bags, he had one person that did a repair, he had a couple of people that actually bought vacuum cleaners while I was there and then I can't remember what the other person was but you would want to keep track of all that.

If you have a good system, for the person that bought bags you may be able to put the style number of that bag with their information and then if you have some sort of automation built into your system if they bought them today and the average person needs vacuum bags every 3 months, 3 months from now you might want to send them a reminder and maybe give them 10 percent off if they come in within 10 days or whatever it might be to create a little bit of urgency there. When you segment your list it leaves you open to other opportunities to go after that.

The lawn care company also does pest control but they had a very small percentage of their customers that were using them for pest control. We created a list of all the customers who didn't have pest control. It was a pretty big list and we started marketing pest control to those people. We did other things as well but we also made sure that every month something that we sent them would include something about pest control, it was not always offers, and it might be educational material just to let people know.

In the survey we did at the lawn care company we asked people if they knew all of the services we offered. There were people who didn't know that we offered those services and just because of the survey knowledge and their relationship with the company they added the services. They called and requested the services because they liked us already and they didn't know that we did that. That shows how having a great list and using it correctly can get you the kind of business that you want, you do a survey and you get business from it.

Any way that you can segment your list, certainly you want to do it. If you have a list of customers and prospects you want to segment the 2 so you can do different things with the prospects and the customers. You always want to at least make sure you have that. I may have a customer in my business that only does social media marketing with me but there may be an opportunity to do a website or Infusionsoft or Constant Contact, so I can know those things as well.

The more that I know the more I can create offers specifically for different groups of people. It helps build niches and as Dan Kennedy says the riches are in the niches. If you can build niches of customers and you can market directly to them you can usually make a little bit more money, charge a little bit more, make a little bit more money for a product.

Susan: I think that's a great example of how to leverage multiple smaller lists.

Chris: That's where having it in something like Constant Contact or another online tool or app can help. I didn't talk about apps at all but our app has kind of been around a long time, there are still lots of people who use it out there. If you have something, you can segment your list many, many different ways and they have that opportunity versus if you're just doing it in Excel. I've seen people try to keep their list in Outlook and there are ways to set up categories and all within Outlook but it's probably not the most efficient way to do it and it doesn't give you nearly the flexibility other tools will allow you to have.

How to Avoid Common Mistakes When Creating Your Customer List...

Susan: What are some of the mistakes you see business owners make when building a list?

Chris: I think one of the big mistakes that I see people making is they get a list of names they don't know and they'll essentially spam the list. They'll go out and buy a list and it'll have email addresses on it and they'll put it into Constant Contact and they'll try to email these people and then they'll get spam complaints and they'll get shut off and in the end they'll be less productive. You're not going to be able to get away with that today. I'm not an expert on spam laws but I know you can't email a business, or really anyone you don't have a business relationship with. When you start emailing people you don't know you leave yourself open to legal action and it could certainly hurt your credibility in the business world.

People make mistakes when they're accumulating their list. They may not segment like they should and then they learn after 6 months that they should have segmented this way versus that way and that's where you're just going to have to change. It is water under the bridge at that point, just try to make it better from that point on. As I said I have about 2,700 people on my list and we have 400 top prospects, which is about 15 percent of our list and we do direct mail to those 400. If you think about segmenting customers and prospects, and then maybe rating your prospects as 1, 2 or 3, having that information segmented correctly is very helpful and you'll learn to do it better as you go along. The important thing at this stage is to start so you have something to eventually segment. This list is where I get many new customers.

Another mistake I see is if you're planning to have any sort of decent sized list you need to start with some sort of technology solution that's going to give you some flexibility. Use either an online solution like Constant Contact or Infusionsoft. You can start with Excel but you're better off starting with something more robust. It is such an important part of a business, investing a little bit of money to do it right will be a great investment.

Dan Kennedy says "good is good enough". Too often people wait to have the ultimate email template to send out to their list. They spend over two months designing a template when they could get the same results with a simple text based email without all of the graphics and decorations.

No matter what your politics, you should check out the results of the Obama campaign fundraising emails. They found the best headline that generated the most donations for them was a simple "HEY!" subject line. People would click on it and it would say we need your support, click here to give us money. That short email was one of the most successful emails in history. I think they raised close to $5 million with this one email. Stalling to make it perfect and not sending out emails is probably another big mistake I see. Sending a text based email versus trying to do a fancy email can be more effective. Get your list started and send them an email about your product or service. Avoid perfection paralysis at all costs. Don't go into grid lock trying to make things perfect.

How to Successfully Grow Your Customer List...

Susan: Very helpful Chris. Just get started! Let's talk about how the business owner can grow their list.

Chris: One strategy is to do an endorsement for a business in your industry. For example, let's say I was a sprinkler company and I have a thousand customers on my list where I turn on and off their sprinkler system every year and I add 100 new sprinkler customers every year. Look for a closely related business that you can partner up with. So for our example, maybe you contact a local lawn service company. The lawn service wouldn't necessarily take the list from the sprinkler company but maybe the sprinkler company owner would partner with the lawn service and say I know you have a sprinkler system and it's clear you've invested a lot in your lawn. I know a lawn service company who does a great job that will make sure between the lawn service and your sprinkler system you'll have the best looking lawn in the neighborhood. You would write an endorsement letter and the lawn service would get new customers from the sprinklers company's customers and vice versa.

Susan: You find companies that are in related businesses?

Chris: Right. Another example of this is people who do weddings. There are a lot of products and services which could work together to cross-pollinate. If someone needs a DJ for a wedding they are probably also going to need a venue or a minister or someone to do their makeup and hair. The list is endless. You could find other partners and when somebody comes in they could partner with them and offer a service the client may be in need of. Find complementary businesses and try to leverage that part of your list together so both parties grow their list.

Here's Exactly How to Get Started Leveraging Your List...

Susan: What can you do for someone who wants to start a list, what are the different ways they can work with you Chris?

Chris: Folks can work with us on a project basis. For example, if they are a company and they want to start building their list we could help them set up the list in Constant Contact. If they have an existing list we could import it into Constant Contact and help them set up a form on their website to capture client information. If they have a physical storefront we could help them with guest books or another way people are capturing information is to have an iPad where people can enter in their information right there at the counter. We can help them within their store to set it up so it's automated and easy.

The biggest advantage, as we stated, is we help people create the construct for building the list they need and we show them how to use their list to grow their business. Once you start collecting the list, that's just the beginning. The exciting part is to start using the list to get more sales; that's where our strength is, helping business owners use their list to get more business. We show them tactics and strategies to do that. The results are always 3x, 5x, and even 10x the investment.

Susan: If someone had questions or needed more information from you Chris how can they get in touch with you?

Chris: They can email me at cripley@smg2.com or call my cell at 301-328-2113.

Susan: Thanks so much for sharing this with us Chris. This can be the difference between a business thriving or as you've pointed out, declining or even going out of business.

Chris: Thanks Susan, I'm passionate about helping these business owners to create their list. I've seen the positive compounding effect it has on their business.

Here's How to Grow Your Small Business by Leveraging Your Customer List...

You already know how to run a successful small business. The confusing part is not knowing how to automate and leverage your customer list to increase your sales.

That's where we come in. We help people just like you leverage their customer list to grow their business.

Here are 3 ways I can help you right now...

Step 1: Join my mailing list and receive access to my video series on leveraging your list. Visit ChrisRipley.com to sign up.

Step 2: Hire me to work with you to grow your list and boost your sales.

Step 3: Hire me to do Constant Contact or Infusionsoft consulting for your business.

Most people think it takes thousands of dollars of advertising to grow their small business.

Now you can grow your small business for a fraction of the cost.

If you'd like us to help, just send an email to: cripley@smg2.com and we will take it from there.

About the Author

Chris Ripley spent 22 years in retail sales and marketing with Macy's, Dayton-Hudson, and May Company. He was a women's shoe buyer for 4 years and a store manager of 14 years. He also spent two years as Senior Director of Development at the College of Southern Maryland.

Currently Chris is the owner of the Strategic Marketing Group, a Waldorf, Maryland, based marketing and business development firm. He helps companies separate themselves from the competition and eliminate them. The company uses direct marketing, video marketing, social media marketing, and local search. He also is an adjunct professor at the College of Southern Maryland and the University of Phoenix.

Chris earned a B.A. in Economics from the University of Virginia in 1981, and received his M.S. in Management with a concentration in Marketing from the University of Maryland University College in 2005.